THE BATTLE OF THE LITTLE BIGHORN

🔥 Little Bighorn National Monument in South Dakota is now a popular tourist site. Thousands of people visit the national park each year to see where the famous battle took place.

THE BATTLE
OF THE
LITTLE
BIGHORN

STEVE THENUISSEN

MASON CREST PUBLISHERS

Mason Crest Publishers
370 Reed Road
Broomall PA 19008
www.masoncrest.com

First printing

1 3 5 7 9 8 6 4 2

Library of Congress Cataloging-in-Publication Data
on file at the Library of Congress

ISBN 1-59084-065-8

Publisher's note: many of the quotations in this book come from
original sources, and contain the spelling and grammatical
inconsistencies of the original text.

CONTENTS

👆 The chaos of Custer's last stand is shown in this painting, titled "Call of the Bugle." Lieutenant Colonel George A. Custer underestimated the strength of the Native American force he attacked, and the Sioux and Cheyenne warriors crushed the U.S. Seventh Cavalry in July 1876.

DEATH IN THE AFTERNOON

THE DUST AND SMOKE HUNG HEAVY IN THE AIR.
SEVEN MEN, CHOKING AND CURSING, STRAINED
their watery eyes through the haze to make out the enemy
ahead. As they frantically worked to reload and fire their
Springfield rifles, these last remaining Seventh Cavalry
troopers may have prayed to their God for deliverance.

A little over an hour earlier they had been confident and
strong, riding in the midst of the proud Seventh Cavalry and
looking toward another victory over the Indians. But now the
Seventh had been ripped apart. Its famous leader, George A.
Custer, was dead, and the entire command was within a
whisker of total destruction. How it had happened didn't
matter now. These men, grouped around a tattered Seventh
Cavalry flag, only cared about surviving.

Survival was also on the minds of the thousands of
Indian warriors who swarmed over the battlefield toward
these last living **cavalry** soldiers. On that Sunday afternoon,
survival brought the tribes together into the largest Indian
village that the West had ever seen. And it was survival that

The Springfield rifle, used by the American soldiers at the battle of the Little Bighorn, was a .30-caliber bolt-action rifle manufactured in Springfield, Massachusetts.

had brought them pouring out of that village earlier in the afternoon with war cries. Like bees swarming out of a hive, the Indians closed in on Custer's column.

The soldiers had immediately gone from attack to defense. As the dust cloud of the approaching Indians overtook the soldiers, they became confused and were soon surrounded. Lieutenant Colonel Custer gave the order to dismount. The Seventh Cavalry flag was driven into the dusty ground as the bugler sounded out the dismount order. Fear and determination showed on the faces of the men as they took their positions and waited for the enemy attack on what has come to be known as Custer Hill.

The first Indian charge unleashed a hail of arrows and bullets upon the soldiers. Men screamed out as they were hit. Yet the return fire from the rifles of the soldiers drove back the charge. Then the Indians came again. More deadly fire rained in upon the soldiers. By now the dust from the horses had mixed with the smoke from the gunfire to rob the soldiers of their vision. They stumbled about like blind men as the Indians' bullets and arrows tore into them. The soldiers' horses, which were being held by the reins by

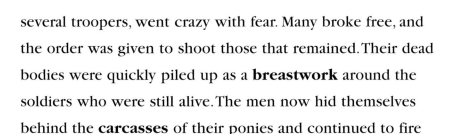

several troopers, went crazy with fear. Many broke free, and the order was given to shoot those that remained. Their dead bodies were quickly piled up as a **breastwork** around the soldiers who were still alive. The men now hid themselves behind the **carcasses** of their ponies and continued to fire upon the Indians.

As several hundred Indians made their way up the hill to fight the soldiers face to face, hundreds more stayed back and let loose their arrows. They shot their bows in a wide curve in the sky, to have the arrows fall with a deadly thud amongst the troopers.

Many of the soldiers soon ran out of ammunition for their rifles. Throwing them aside, they reached for their Colt revolvers, desperately trying to continue fighting. But the Indians were almost upon the troopers. The soldiers fired more quickly, but the Indians kept coming. The war cries of the warriors drowned out the cursing of the white men. Now the warriors were too close for guns. Soldiers swung their rifles like baseball bats as a last defense. But it was no use. In hand-to-hand combat, the outnumbered soldiers were killed one by one.

Just seven remained—grouped around their symbol of unity, the Seventh Cavalry flag. Their hands were hot from holding their overworked Springfield rifles, their faces, dripping with sweat, were caked with dust—yet they

George Armstrong Custer was born in the little village of Rumley, Ohio, on December 5, 1839. As a child George, whose family called him Autie, was full of fun. When he was about five years old, he decided he wanted to be a soldier. At the Young Men's Academy in Monroe, Michigan, he smuggled military books into class and read them behind his textbooks.

When he was 17, George was admitted to the United States Military Academy at West Point. Over the next three years he consistently ranked at the bottom of his class. However, he graduated in June 1861—just in time for the Civil War.

During the course of the war, he proved a man who was a failure in the classroom could be a success on the battlefield. He won many distinctions for bravery, and by the war's end he had gained the rank of major general. At age 23, he was the youngest man to ever achieve that rank in the United States army.

After the war Custer was sent out West, where he served as a lieutenant colonel of the Seventh Cavalry. In 1868, the Seventh Cavalry attacked an Indian village on the Washita River, killing more than 100 Indians and taking many prisoners. Six years later, Custer led the Seventh into the sacred Black Hills, where gold was discovered. It was this discovery that led to the war for the Black Hills and the battle of the Little Bighorn—where Custer's luck finally ran out.

continued to fight. But now the entire Indian force turned on them, thousands of warriors gathering for the kill. With knives and tomahawks drawn, they closed in on the last of these intruders who dared to invade the Indians' homeland.

To the Sioux, the Black Hills—which they called Paha Sapa—were sacred ground, a place where the spirits of their dead warriors could rest so their eyes would become accustomed to beauty before they entered into paradise. Young warriors were also sent to the hills to seek the Great Spirit of Wakan Tanka, who would guide their futures.

2
GOLD IN THE BLACK HILLS

ON THE BORDER BETWEEN THE STATES OF SOUTH DAKOTA AND WYOMING LIE THE Black Hills. This mountain range covers an area of about 6,000 square miles. To white people, the Black Hills held no special value, and in an 1868 treaty the United States government was more than willing to give the Hills over to the Native Americans.

The treaty clearly kept white people out of the Hills. In part it read: "No white person or persons shall be permitted to settle upon or occupy any portion of the territory, or without the consent of the Indians to pass through the same."

For the Sioux it was vitally important to keep the whites well away from the Hills. More than just a mountain range, to them the Black Hills, which they called Paha Sapa, was the center of their world. It was the dwelling place of gods, the home of sacred power—the most holy ground. The Hills were also a rich source of food, shelter, and security.

👆 This photograph, taken in 1874, shows the supply wagons for Custer's expedition into the Black Hills. Custer was sent to protect gold prospectors in the region—even though the U.S. government had promised not to enter the Sioux's sacred lands.

According to Standing Elk, an Oglala Sioux who camped alongside Sitting Bull, "Indians would rove all around, but when they were in need of something they could just go in there and get it."

In the early 1870s, however, rumors began to go around nearby towns that the Black Hills contained gold. Explorers and **prospectors** who had sneaked their way into the Hills told stories of fabulous amounts of the shiny metal, much of it simply lying in the grass ready to be picked up. Settlers along the edges of the Great Sioux Reservation, which included the Black Hills, looked to the mountains with envious eyes. Ignoring the Fort Laramie Treaty of 1868, some of them went into the sacred hills in search of their fortune. When the Indians found these intruders, they either killed the intruders or chased them out.

In May 1874, the army decided that it needed to do something about the Black Hills problem, and an expedition to the Hills was decided upon. The official objective of the expedition was to survey the land and decide the best place for a military post. But there was another, more immediate, reason for this mission, as was revealed in a telegram message from Lieutenant General Philip Sheridan to the man who would lead the expedition, Lieutenant Colonel George Custer:

Prepare at once to outfit an Expedition to the Black Hills to investigate rumours of large gold deposits & survey area for possible establishment of Military Posts.

In July 1874, Lieutenant Colonel Custer marched out of the newly built Fort Abraham Lincoln at the head of the proud Seventh Cavalry. With him were over 1,000 men, including two prospectors and three newspaper correspondents.

The 110 wagons provided all of the necessary equipment, and the soldiers were looking forward to an enjoyable mission. They, too, had heard of the wonders to be found in the Black Hills—plenty of game for hunting and plenty of gold for fortune making. After spending months cooped up at Fort Lincoln, the exploration into the Black Hills seemed like a grand adventure.

From the hilltops, the Sioux Indians watched as the long **columns** of soldiers invaded their sacred lands. The Sioux were not happy. Oglala Sioux Chief Red Cloud said, "I do not like General Custer and all his soldiers going into the Black Hills as that is the country of the Oglala Sioux."

The Sioux chief Red Cloud was a strong and respected leader. Angered by the construction of forts in Sioux land, he waged a brutal war against the white soldiers. The U.S. eventually signed a peace treaty at Fort Laramie in 1868; the government agreed to abandon three forts and to keep settlers out of the Black Hills. However, Custer's expedition six years later violated the treaty.

The Sioux, who had given Custer the name Long Hair, now had a new name for him—the Chief of Thieves. The trail that Custer's wagons had made into the middle of the Black Hills became known as the Thieves' Road. Yet the Indians did not try to stop the advancing columns as they snaked their way into the Hills.

People searching for gold in riverbeds were often said to be panning. As they looked for gold nuggets, they tipped the gravel from the river back and forth in a pan to separate the ordinary gravel from the gold.

The soldiers found that the Black Hills were like an unspoiled paradise. The air was clear, the water was pure, and game was plenty. Custer and his men set up a permanent camp on French Creek, right in the middle of the Hills, and set off exploring and hunting. Custer himself fell in love with the area. He later wrote that his days in the Black Hills were among the happiest of his life. During one hunt he managed to kill a hunter's greatest prize—a grizzly bear.

On July 30, Horatio Ross, one of the two miners in the party, found traces of gold in a streambed. Then more gold was found. By August 15, Custer was able to write a report to General Alfred Terry stating:

On some of the water courses almost every panful of earth produced gold in small, but paying, quantities . . . the miners report that they found gold among the roots of the grass.

Sitting Bull was born in South Dakota in 1831. He was a member of the Hunkpapa band of Sioux. His father named him Slow, and he kept that name until the age of 14, when he joined a raid on the enemy of the Sioux, the Crow Indians. There Slow showed himself to be brave in the face of the enemy. From then on he came to be known by the adult name Sitting Bull.

As he grew into manhood, Sitting Bull discovered he was able to see visions. He became a medicine man as well as a war chief of his people. At the battle of the Little Bighorn, Sitting Bull was chief over the entire Indian village. He did not, however, take part in the fighting; instead he protected the women and children in the village. After the battle, Sitting Bull moved to Canada. After four years he returned to America where he was put on a reservation. Sitting Bull was killed in 1890.

The news of the gold discovery spread like wildfire. Newspapers made the announcement in bold print—GOLD IN THE HILLS. It didn't take long for the gold diggers to gather. Before Custer's expedition had even returned to Fort Lincoln, parties of fortune seekers were preparing to head into the Hills. Not caring that the land belonged to the Indians, these men couldn't wait to begin panning and digging for their fortune.

Within six months, the Black Hills were filled with gold-crazy white men. Sioux chiefs on the **reservations** protested to the government that this was illegal and must be stopped. In response, General George Crook went into the Hills to see just how many prospectors he could find. Within a short time he had found over 1,000 men. But rather than forcing them out, he simply told them that they were breaking the law and left them to continue.

The army knew it could not stop this white invasion. So rather than trying to uphold the rights of the Indians, the government sent a peace **commission** to try to buy the Black Hills from them.

🔥 As a Union general during the Civil War, Ulysses S. Grant had forced the rebellious states of the south to surrender. As president, Grant hoped to expand the nation into Sioux lands—even though the Fort Laramie Treaty of 1868 granted the Sioux control of the Black Hills forever.

THE GATHERING STORM

IN AUGUST 1875, A HANDFUL OF POLITICIANS, ARMY OFFICERS, AND MISSIONARIES RODE INTO the Red Cloud Sioux Indian Agency to buy the Black Hills. They had been sent by the government to sort out the Black Hills problem. Senator William B. Allison was the chairman of this group. Messages had been sent to all of the Sioux Indians who lived outside of the reservation to invite them to a meeting to talk about the Black Hills. Most of the chiefs, however, refused to even talk about selling the Hills. Sitting Bull said to the messenger who came to invite him to the meeting, "I want you to go and tell the great father that I do not want to sell any land to the government." Then he grabbed some dirt from the ground and added, "Not even as much as this."

All of the other chiefs agreed with Sitting Bull. Still, they decided to send some warriors to the meeting to watch what was happening. About 400 Indians from outside the reservation traveled to the meeting. They joined about 10,000 Indians who lived on the reservation, as well as many from other

In 1868, U.S. government leaders promised the Sioux that they would not take the Black Hills in a treaty meeting at Fort Laramie, Wyoming.

reservations. So when Senator Allison and his men arrived at the meeting place, they were met by a large gathering of Indians.

Senator Allison and his men did not have an easy job. The Fort Laramie Treaty of 1868, which had given the Black Hills to the Indians, made clear the terms for getting the land back: at least three quarters of the adult male Native Americans who were interested in the land would have to agree to sell it. But when the white men looked out over the sea of angry and determined warriors camped before them, they knew that they would not be able to achieve this.

When the Sioux spoke of the "great father," they meant the president of the United States.

From the start, the meeting went badly. Just as Senator Allison rose to welcome the Indians, a cloud of dust rose in the distance, and a band of warriors came charging toward the whites. These warriors were painted for battle and carried rifles. They galloped toward the **commissioners** and then suddenly swerved to form a circle around them as they fired their rifles into the sky and made loud whooping sounds. Then another band of Native Americans approached on horseback and did the same thing, forming a circle outside the first one. Others followed, and before long more than a 1,000 armed warriors surrounded the camp.

The white commissioners were nervous at this show of strength from the Indians. Senator Allison decided that they would be wasting their time to try to buy the Black Hills when the Indians were in such a dangerous mood. So he changed his tactics. Instead, he asked the chiefs for permission to take gold from the area in exchange for money. He knew that the Indians placed little value on the shiny metal that was so important to the white man. But to the Indians this was not acceptable. They wanted the whites out of the hills and that was final!

The commissioners told the chiefs that the government was unable to keep the gold miners out of the hills. If the Indians did not allow them in, said Senator Allison, there would be great trouble. After much angry talk, the chiefs went off by themselves to discuss the matter. After three days they again met with the commissioners. As they prepared to give their speeches, a rider on a gray horse rode up to the assembled commissioners. He was Little Big Man and he had been sent by the great war chief Crazy Horse. He was wearing war paint and had two guns in his belt. From atop his horse he yelled to the chiefs, "I will kill the first chief who speaks for selling the Black Hills!"

None of them did.

The commissioners packed up and headed back to Washington to report to President Grant. Senator Allison told the government that the only way to get the Black Hills was to force the Native Americans to sell them, and if that didn't work, to take them off the Hills anyway. But none of the white men in Washington understood just how important the Black Hills were to the Sioux Indians.

The president of the United States, however, knew he had a problem. Gold fever was driving thousands of prospectors to the Black Hills. But the Hills belonged to the Native Americans, and by the winter of 1875, even President Grant understood that they were not willing to give up the Hills without a fight. Grant had been a hero during the Civil War, but he had no

👆 The Sioux leaders Sitting Bull and Crazy Horse, shown here in the center of a group of warriors, were among the chiefs who opposed the sale of the Black Hills to the United States.

experience in fighting Native Americans. Yet to Grant's military mind, the only way out of the corner into which he saw himself being backed was to go to war against the Indians. A campaign against the "hostile" Indians who lived outside the reservations should be enough to frighten into submission both those who lived outside the reservations and the thousands who lived at the reservations. Then, Grant reasoned, the Indians would be only too happy to sign over the Black Hills.

So President Grant made up his mind to take the Black Hills by force. But he had to make it look as if the Indians started the fight. That way the public wouldn't be able to blame him for attacking the Indians, who had remained peaceful all through the Black Hills situation. The president decided upon a two-step plan. First, he would stop the army from holding back miners who wanted to go into the Hills in search of gold. This would make the Indians angrier as they saw more and more white men flooding into their sacred country. If they attacked the miners, the president would have a reason to strike back. The second part of the president's plan was to give the so-called hostile Indians who lived outside of the reservations a deadline for coming into the reservations. If they didn't, they would be considered to be at war with the United States.

A deadline of January 31, 1876, was set for the "hostile" Indians to come into the reservations. In late December, messengers were sent out from the reservations to find the bands of Indians who were in their winter camps in the mountains. But the winter that year was especially harsh. The snow was heavy, blizzards swept across the hills, and it was hard for the messengers to find the winter camps; many of them only got there within days of the January 31 deadline. Even if they had wanted, the camped men, women, and children could not have reached the reservation by the deadline.

The chiefs, however, did not want to go to the reservation anyway, and they chose to ignore the demands. They told the messengers that if they decided to come into the reservation, they would do so in the springtime. The Indians did not share the whites' idea of time. To them it meant nothing to have to be somewhere by a certain date, and they were puzzled to see

Crazy Horse was born into the Lakota or Western band of Sioux Indians around 1840. As a child, he was known as Curly. At age 12, Curly had a vision of a painted warrior riding on a yellow warhorse and leading his people to victory. Following behind the warrior was a black hawk. Curly knew that the warrior was himself. It was then that he took on the name Crazy Horse. Whenever he went into battle, Crazy Horse would paint himself with marks of lightning and wear a black hawk in his hair. This seemed to give him power well beyond what was normal.

In the wars with the United States army, there were just two battles where all the white men were killed—the Fetterman massacre and the battle of the Little Bighorn. Crazy Horse led the Indians both times. In 1877 Crazy Horse surrendered to the U.S. army. A few months later, though, he was killed at Fort Robinson, South Dakota.

the messengers make so much effort in the bitter cold winter to deliver this strange message. Then they shrugged off the message and went back to their winter camp duties. They didn't know that it was all part of the government's plan to rob them of their sacred place, Paha Sapa.

To the government the deadline was serious. By January 31, 1876, none of the "hostiles" had come into the reservations. The next day in Washington, the problem of what to do about these Native Americans was formally handed by the Department of Indian Affairs to the War Department. Immediately, plans were put in place for a campaign to hunt down the Indians while they were still in their winter camps. The army would teach them a lesson they would never forget.

Sitting Bull rides at the head of a war party. Many of the Sioux refused to leave their homelands and move to the reservations created for them by the U.S. government. As a result, the army was sent after them to force the Native Americans onto reservations.

4
CENTENNIAL CAMPAIGN

BY FEBRUARY OF 1876, THE UNITED STATES ARMY
WAS PREPARING ITSELF FOR A MAJOR ATTACK ON
the Sioux Indian Nation. As these plans came together, however,
the Sioux Indians themselves camped peacefully in the hills of
Montana. They knew nothing of the plans being drawn against
them. These Indians called themselves Lakota and were divided
into seven bands. These were the Oglala, Brule, Northern
Cheyennes, Hunkpapa, Mineconjou, Blackfoot, and Cut-Head
bands. The Hunkpapa band, led by Sitting Bull, and the Oglala
band, led by Crazy Horse, made up the largest numbers. About
3,500 hostile Indians refused to come in and live on the
reservations. About 1,000 warriors were included in this number.

For the Sioux warrior, the showing of bravery and
cunning in warfare was the highest honor. At about the age of
15, a male would enter his first battle, and a man would
continue to be a warrior until he had a son old enough to
fight and represent his family in battle. If he had no son at the
time of reaching the retirement age from warfare—about
37—he would adopt a son. Each group of warriors had a
chief, but he did not lead the men in the same way army

General George Crook was one of the Army's top Indian fighters. After fighting the Sioux and Cheyenne in the Black Hills, Crook would go on to lead troops in the southwest against the Apaches and their bold leader, Geronimo.

generals did. In Indian warfare there was no commander. The warriors fought the way they wanted to, each one deciding how best to show his bravery. A warrior's bravery in battle was shown by the risks he took. For example, to touch the body of an enemy was a sign of bravery, but it was no honor to kill a man. Better to touch him with a light stick (called a coup stick), the Sioux believed, and therefore insult his manliness. In fact, if a Sioux killed an enemy with a bullet or an arrow, honor would go to the first man to race up to the body and touch the fallen body, not to the one who had done the killing.

Each Indian band had its own warrior societies. These were groups of young men who tried to outdo other warrior societies in battle.

Obviously, the whites looked at fighting from a very different perspective. General Philip Sheridan was the commanding officer of the Military Division of Missouri. His area of control included the Black Hills, and this made him responsible for carrying out the order to attack the Sioux. Sheridan wanted to move against the Indians straightaway. In the wintertime the Sioux found it harder to move around and they could be more easily surprised. So, on February 8, Sheridan sent messages to General Alfred Terry, commander of the Department of the Dakota, and General George Crook, Commander of the Department of the Platte, instructing them to get ready to take to the field.

But there were problems. As a part of General Terry's forces, the Seventh Cavalry was to march from Fort Abraham Lincoln. But the commanding officer, Lieutenant Colonel Custer, was stuck in Washington, appearing as a witness in a court case. Custer was the army's most experienced Indian fighter, and Terry did not want to go into battle without him. Reports had also come in that the Indians were not camped where the generals had thought them to be. Rather than being on the Little Missouri River, they had moved toward the Yellowstone. This meant they could not be reached by a quick winter march as General Terry had expected. Instead, the campaign would have to wait until the early spring when Custer had returned and the weather had improved to allow a longer march.

The Seventh Cavalry was the only cavalry **regiment** in the eastern Montana area. But in early 1876, it was not ready to take the field. It didn't have enough officers, and 70 of the men were due to be discharged from the army on the May 1. Besides this, many of the troopers were new **recruits** who did not have any experience. Some of them were **immigrants** who could hardly speak English. Others were just out of school and had joined for the excitement of fighting Indians. Then there were those who were criminals trying to avoid the law, along with others who simply needed the money. All of these types of men made up the Seventh Cavalry.

The life of a trooper in the United States cavalry in the 1870s was a mixture of boredom, excitement, and fear. Long months were spent in the fort practicing drills and doing routine jobs. After a while, the soldiers looked forward to getting out in the field and chasing down the enemy. When they did get out on the trail, however, many of these men prayed that they would never see an Indian. They were only too happy to get back to the fort in one piece. Apart from the fear of meeting the enemy, the troopers had to deal with the harsh land over which they traveled, as well as the difficult weather conditions. Snow, bitter cold, and rain in winter balanced scorching, unbearable heat, and dusty windstorms in summer.

Captain Theodore Goldin remembered his first spring night in camp on the 1876 campaign this way: "Early in the night we woke up, our teeth chattering and the very marrow in our bones seemingly congealed. We tried more blankets, but that didn't work, and at last chilled through and through, we crept out of our tents, wrapped a blanket over our overcoats and spent the remainder of the night crouching over the cook fires."

The planned march by the Seventh Cavalry from Fort Abraham Lincoln was delayed by the absence of Custer and the bad weather. However, the forces of General George Crook were right on target as they prepared for the march from their base at Fort Fetterman. On February 29, Crook led 662 troopers and 30 officers of the Second and Third Cavalry and the Fourth Infantry out of Fort Fetterman and north toward the hostile Indians in the Bighorn Mountains. By March 5, the troops had reached the banks of the Powder River. Since leaving Fort Fetterman, they had seen many signs of Indian spies. They knew the enemy watched their every move. General Crook sent scouts out toward the Tongue River to search for Indians. While the scouts were gone, however, the Sioux attacked the main camp. For more than half an hour, they kept constant rifle fire on the soldier camp. And then, suddenly, the Indians disappeared.

For the next few days the soldiers played a frustrating cat-and-mouse game with the Sioux. General Crook became impatient as the enemy outsmarted his every move. On March 16, however, his scouts found the trail to the Indian village on the Powder River. General Crook immediately prepared for attack. At daybreak on March 17, Colonel Joseph Reynolds led 375 soldiers, charging down the banks of the Powder River toward the sleeping village of Northern Cheyennes and Oglala Sioux. As one troop of cavalry galloped into the tepee village from the north, another attacked from the south, while a third took charge of the Indians' horses. The Indians rushed from their tepees and desperately tried to avoid the wild bullets of the soldiers. Soon the 200 warriors in the camp were defending themselves. They managed to hold off the soldiers until the women and children could escape.

The standoff between the soldiers and the Indians lasted until early afternoon. By then, the soldiers had burned the village to the ground and captured the Indians' entire pony herd. The soldiers then pulled out and headed back to their main camp, but that night the Indians managed to recapture their horses. General Crook was angry that the attack had not gone better. The victory that everyone had expected had turned into an embarrassing standoff. Nine days later, Crook's forces returned to Fort Fetterman. Its mission, to attack and destroy the hostile Sioux, had been a bitter failure.

Crazy Horse leads a group of his Oglala warriors in an attack on the cavalry. After Crook's attack on the camp at Powder River, the Sioux realized they needed to fight together in order to defeat the American forces that opposed them.

For the Indians, though, the Battle of Powder River was an important lesson. It told them that the army was serious about its declaration of war. They now knew that they were in for the fight of their lives. Their only chance for survival now was to gather together into one powerful camp—the biggest gathering in their history—and fight the white man as a united force. And so they began to come together.

🔥 Custer was confident that his Seventh Cavalry would rout the Sioux and Cheyenne. He did not listen to his Native American scouts, who warned him about the size of the force the U.S. soldiers were pursuing in the early summer of 1876.

CUSTER'S LUCK

GENERAL SHERIDAN'S PLAN TO ATTACK THE
INDIANS WAS A SIMPLE ONE. THREE COLUMNS
coming from different directions would close in on the Indian
camp. General Crook would come north from Fort Fetterman
in Wyoming. General Gibbon would move east from Fort Ellis
in Montana. And Lieutenant Colonel Custer would move in on
the Indians from Fort Abraham Lincoln in Dakota Territory.
Sheridan believed that any of these three columns could easily
defeat the Indians—together they would totally crush them.

But by the end of March, this plan had already begun to
fall apart when General Crook had met the enemy on the
Powder River and been turned back toward Fort Fetterman. So
there would be no meeting of the three-pronged attack as
planned. General Gibbon set off from Fort Ellis on April 3 with
436 men, but his job now was to prevent the Indians from
escaping to the north. And the Seventh Cavalry under
Lieutenant Colonel Custer was still not ready to take to the
field. Meanwhile, General Crook's army in Wyoming was
reorganizing itself to march toward the hostile Indians again. It
was a period of frustration for Generals Sheridan and Terry as

delays and complications saw the winter campaign drag into a summer campaign.

Not until the end of May did General Sheridan report to President Grant that three offensive forces had taken the field

🖑 Some of the wives, including General Custer's wife Elizabeth, rode along with the troops when they left Fort Abraham Lincoln. The women returned to the fort the next day. At their last good-bye, Elizabeth Custer felt something terrible was going to happen to her husband. "With my husband's departure, my last happy days in garrison were ended, as a premonition of disaster that I had never known before weighed me down," she later wrote. "I could not shake off the baleful influence of depressing thoughts."

to attack and defeat the Indians.
The Seventh Cavalry had finally
marched out of Fort Abraham
Lincoln on May 17. General
Terry himself commanded this
column, with Lieutenant
Colonel Custer riding alongside
him. The occasion was a sad but

The army used trumpet calls
to signal various orders—
for instance, to charge or
retreat—to the men.

exciting one for the soldiers. It was good to get away from the
boredom of the fort—but they were afraid they might never
return. Despite their fears, they proudly marched past the
army wives and children on their way out of the fort.

On June 10, the Terry-Custer column reached the
Yellowstone River. There they met with the supply steamer
Far West. As previously arranged, General Gibbon and his
Montana column were also there. But no one knew what had
happened to General Crook, who was supposed to be
working his way north from Wyoming. Only later would
General Terry learn that Crook had once again fought the
Indians—this time on the Upper Rosebud River—and been
turned back to Wyoming.

On June 14, General Terry sent a scouting party, led by
Major Marcus Reno, to try to locate the Indians. The party
returned six days later with the news that they had come
across a large Indian trail going up Rosebud Creek, between
the Tongue and Bighorn Rivers. With this information, General

Marcus Reno was born in Carrolltown, Illinois, in 1834. After graduating from the U.S. Military Academy at West Point in 1857, he served as a cavalry officer during the Civil War. After the war Reno was posted to the Seventh Cavalry as a major, second in command under Lieutenant Colonel George Custer. Reno was a serious man who did not find it easy to get along with people. After his wife died in 1874, he would get drunk often and end up in fights. Some people thought he acted like a coward during the battle of the Little Bighorn. However, he was cleared of wrongdoing by a military inquiry. After the battle, though, he got in trouble with the army because of his drinking. He was ordered to leave the army in 1880. Marcus Reno died on March 30, 1889.

Terry was now ready to go into action. Custer was ordered to take his Seventh Cavalry up Rosebud Creek and follow the trail that Major Reno had discovered. Meanwhile, Terry himself would go with General Gibbon up the Yellowstone River toward the Little Bighorn Valley. Terry thought that the helpless Indians would be caught between the columns and try to escape south to the Bighorn Mountains. But Custer would be waiting to block off the escape. No one even considered the possibility that the Indians might actually stand and fight.

The Seventh Cavalry left the camp on the Yellowstone River at noon on June 22. They marched about 13 miles up the left bank of the Rosebud River and made camp at around 4 P.M. That evening, Lieutenant Colonel Custer called a meeting of his officers. From now on, he told them, there would be no trumpet calls. The men would get up at 3 A.M. and be marching by 5 A.M. They would cover about 30 miles each day. Even though General Terry had given Custer orders to block the escape of the Indians, his officers knew that he was preparing for war.

The next morning the march got off to a good start. After traveling about eight miles, the column came across an abandoned Indian camp. The camp was large and had only recently been abandoned. From then on the ground was like a plowed field. Lodge pole tracks crisscrossed each other, and the Indian ponies had eaten all the grass. The next day an abandoned Hunkpapa Sioux Sundance Lodge was found. This was where Sitting Bull, just three weeks earlier, had had a vision of dead soldiers falling into his camp. Sitting Bull told the Sioux that this vision showed they would win a great victory.

Custer was now confident that he had the Indians within striking distance. Even though his scouts warned him that there were too many Indians ahead, he was only concerned that they might escape. To prevent this, he ordered a night march for June 24. Ignoring the orders he had received from General Terry, he prepared to attack the Indians on his own.

At 11 P.M. the exhausted soldiers marched the 10 miles up the divide between the Rosebud and Little Bighorn Rivers. At about 2 A.M. they stopped for some much needed sleep. Six hours later, however, they were marching again. At about the time the troopers began to climb back into the saddle, some of Custer's Indian scouts were climbing up a lookout called the Crow's Nest. From here they were able to look down on the Indian village. At first the scouts thought that they were looking down on a series of rolling hills in the Little Bighorn Valley. But then they realized that these never-ending hills were actually horses. It was the largest pony herd they had ever seen. At about 5 A.M. they sent a message back to Custer to come and look for himself.

When Custer reached the lookout, the scouts pointed out the massive pony herd. But even with his binoculars, Custer could not see the horses. The scouts told him that the village was the biggest they had ever come across. He reacted by calling them cowards. The Seventh Cavalry could ride through the entire Sioux Nation, he said. The more Indians there were, the more famous he would become for beating them. He turned away from the scouts and began down the hill back toward the command. But Custer was notified one of the scouts saw a group of Indians moving downstream. To him this could only mean one thing—the Indians had spotted him and were about to make their escape. He had to attack—now.

At about noon Custer had his men marching at a fast trot toward the Indian village. After marching just 15 minutes, though, he stopped the men. He decided to divide his command into three separate units. One **battalion**, under Captain Frederick Benteen, was to scout the hills to the west. Major Reno would take 175 men and attack the Indian village from the southern end. Custer himself, with 221 men, would ride into the village and attack from the north. And so a force that was already greatly outnumbered was split into even smaller pieces. Was Custer pushing his luck just a little too far this time?

The graves of Seventh Cavalry troops mark the spots where the men fell during the battle of the Little Bighorn.

6

INTO HISTORY

THE SUN BEAT DOWN ON THE TIRED TROOPERS OF THE SEVENTH CAVALRY as they advanced over the Montana hills toward their enemy. It was midday on Sunday, June 25, 1876. In just a few days—on the 4th of July—the United States would begin celebrating the biggest party in its history, the **centennial** of its birth. For the man at the head of this column, that was the perfect time for news of a great victory. Lieutenant Colonel Custer hadn't had a victory over the Indians in eight years. Now was his chance once again to shine. Dressed in **buckskins** and wearing a wide-brimmed hat, he was sure that today would mark the turning point of his life.

Others in the column weren't so sure. To Captain Benteen, Custer's order to split the command into three columns was madness. Benteen knew they were facing a massive Indian village and needed to have as large a force as possible together at the time of attack. Major Reno seemed resigned to the idea that they were riding into disaster. The scouts—both

An Oglala Sioux named Amos Bad Heart Bull made this drawing of Crazy Horse shooting down Seventh Cavalry troopers during the battle.

Indians and white men—were convinced that they would all die that day. As for the hundreds of troopers trudging along under that hot summer heat, they knew only that they were marching toward trouble. They had all heard the scouts' reports of the size of the Indian village. Yet they tried to be brave and not think of what could go wrong. After all, they were the Seventh Cavalry.

At 12 minutes after noon, the command divided. Benteen took Companies D, H, and K and began moving toward the **bluffs** to scout for fleeing Indians. Major Reno, with Companies A, G, and M marched along one side of the Sundance River.

Custer, with Companies C, E, F, I, and L rode along the other side of the river. After approximately nine miles, the soldiers saw a dust cloud about five miles ahead of them. To Custer this meant that the Indians were fleeing. He sent a message across the river to Reno telling him to charge toward the attack, promising that his troops would back them up.

History tells us that none of the Seventh Cavalry soldiers under Custer survived the battle of the Little Bighorn. There was one survivor, however. The horse ridden by Captain Myles Keough, named Comanche, was badly wounded in the battle but was lovingly nursed back to health. Comanche died in 1891.

Reno's men now picked up the pace, trotting toward the Little Bighorn River. Having crossed the river, he reformed his troops into battle formation and ordered them to gallop toward the village, which lay about three miles ahead. Indians began coming from the village—on foot and on horseback—to challenge the soldiers. Then, from out of a shallow ravine, hundreds of warriors swarmed toward the invading soldiers. Reno ordered his men to stop and dismount.

The soldiers were caught by surprise. Weren't they meant to be attacking these Indians? Reno ordered every fourth man to take four horses and take cover in a timber stand near the river. The 80 or so men remaining formed a line, each man about nine feet from his companion. They fired

Custer's last stand was a total disaster for the Custer family. As well as losing George, the Custers had four other family members snatched from them on that day. George's two brothers, Boston and Tom, along with his nephew, Henry Armstrong Reed, and his brother-in-law, James Calhoun, were all killed in the battle.

their rifles wildly, even though the Indians were not yet within range. Reno prayed that Custer would appear soon to back him up as promised. The Indians were soon upon the soldiers, forcing them to bunch into a circle. Reno now ordered the men to make a dash for the timber stand. In just a few minutes, his charge deteriorated from an attack to a mad rush for survival.

The troopers fought for their lives in the woods for about half an hour. The Indians soon set the underbrush on fire, forcing men into the open where they would be shot down. Reno's men were getting cut to pieces. He had to do something. He ordered the men to mount their horses and head to the bluffs on the far side of the river. But many didn't hear the order and precious moments were lost in confusion. Suddenly, a bullet smashed into the head of Bloody Knife, a scout who was standing next to Reno. Blood and brains splattered across the Major's face. This greatly unnerved him. He now ordered the men to dismount. As they followed this order, though, he changed his mind and ordered them to remount. His own horse

Frederick Benteen was born on August 23, 1834, in Petersburg, Virginia. Although Virginia was a part of the South, Frederick joined the Union army during the Civil War. He gained a reputation as a brave soldier, and after the war was assigned to the Seventh Cavalry with the rank of captain. This meant Benteen was third in command, after Custer and Reno. He never got along well with Custer, though, and by the time of the battle of the Little Bighorn, the two men hated each other. After the battle, Benteen was involved in several other campaigns against the Indians. He retired from the army in 1888. Two years later he died.

rushed forward in a blind panic once he had mounted. His men charged after him.

The desperate soldiers now galloped for more than a mile along the river toward a high bluff on the other side. Because they had no covering fire, the Indians were able to cut them down as they fled. Then Reno plunged his horse into the water. The others followed. But the Native Americans were close behind. They were able to pull soldiers down from their horses and then kill them with their clubs. Those that made it across the river now scrambled up what has come to be called Reno Hill. So far 40 men had been killed and 13 wounded. The survivors fell down exhausted at the top of the hill and waited for the Indians to close in.

But the Indians did not make that final charge. A few were firing at Reno's men from a distance, but most of them were turning around and charging back to the Indian village. The soldiers on the hill could hear the sound of firing. *It must be Custer*, they may have thought. *He has come to our rescue, after all.* Not long after this, Reno saw Benteen and his three companies approaching. He rushed out to meet the captain, relieved beyond measure that some sort of help had arrived. So two of the divisions that Custer had made just a few hours earlier were now back together. But where was the third? What had happened to Custer?

After Reno had charged off toward the village, Custer had turned to the right. It was his plan to attack the village from the north. At about three o'clock, at a high point along the bluffs Custer got his first look at the Indian village. What he saw there must been a shock to him—a village stretching out for miles with enough lodges for thousands of warriors. This was not what he had expected. From his high point he could also see that Reno's advance had been turned around. But now was no time for regrets. He had an attack of his own to make.

Custer sent two messengers back in search of Benteen, demanding that he bring reinforcements as well as the ammunition packs. He then continued downstream toward the village. As he prepared to cross the Little Bighorn River and plow into the northern end of the Indian village, the warriors came out to meet him. The Indians swarmed toward the invaders. Custer's men were turned back before they reached the river. The Indians drove them downstream, but they were able to reach high ground where Custer quickly organized his men for the battle. He ordered L and I Companies to dismount and form a defense for the rear of the command as he continued to climb the hill.

Although the battle of the Little Bighorn was a great victory for the Sioux and Cheyenne, the Native Americans were fighting a losing war against the westward expansion of the United States.

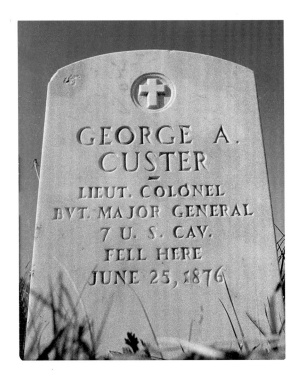

GEORGE A. CUSTER
LIEUT. COLONEL
BVT. MAJOR GENERAL
7 U. S. CAV.
FELL HERE
JUNE 25, 1876

Custer's grave is marked on the battlefield; there is also a memorial to the members of the Seventh Cavalry who fell at the Little Bighorn (pictured on the opposite page). A monument to the Native Americans who fought in the battle is being built.

But now Crazy Horse, the fearless and tactically brilliant war leader of the Oglala Sioux, joined the battle. With hundreds of warriors, Crazy Horse climbed the hill that Custer's men were trying to get to the top of from the opposite side. These Indians were soon spilling over the hill and charging toward Custer's men from the rear. The soldiers were now surrounded. Custer had his men dismount and fight back-to-back for a final stand.

Custer's men fought bravely and desperately. The positions in which their bodies were found tell us that Custer had placed his men well. But the odds against them were too great. By 4:45 P.M. the battlefield was silent. His luck had finally run out. Custer's last stand was over.

The death of Custer and his men electrified and angered the nation. Newspapers in the East received word of the battle just after the Fourth of July holiday. The U.S. Army vowed to avenge Custer's death, and new troops soon streamed across the plains in search of the Sioux and Cheyenne.

By early 1877, most of the Indians had been forced onto reservations. Crazy Horse continued to hold out until May of that year, when he agreed to settle on the Red Cloud

Reservation. However, Crazy Horse was restless, and left the reservation in September. When he returned, he was killed by guards at Fort Robinson, South Dakota.

Sitting Bull also continued to resist. He led a group of Sioux north across the border into Canada. However, the Sioux were unhappy far away from the plains and buffalo that had been central to their way of life. In 1881, they returned to the United States and agreed to settle on reservations.

During the years after the battle of the Little Bighorn, U.S. soldiers helped to put down Native American uprisings throughout the country. The Indian Wars gradually ended as the whites disarmed the tribes and forced them onto reservations. One of the last bands to surrender was the Apaches, under their bold and wily leader Geronimo, who gave up in 1886.

By 1890, a new religion had inspired the Sioux and Cheyenne living on the reservations. They believed that by participating in a ceremony called the Ghost Dance, the spirits of their ancestors would rise, the whites would leave the plains, and the buffalo would return. Fearing that Sitting Bull, who was still a respected chief, would lead an uprising, the army sent soldiers to arrest him in December 1890. There was a struggle, and the chief was shot to death. A short time later, a group of about 350 Sioux left the reservation, afraid they would be attacked by the U.S. Army. Several cavalry units—including the Seventh Cavalry—caught up with them at

Wounded Knee Creek. Although the Sioux leader, Chief Big Foot, was flying a white flag of surrender, on the morning of December 29 the soldiers attacked the Native Americans, killing more than 150 of them. The era of native resistance to the white man was over.

The battle of the Little Bighorn was important because it caused the United States to step up its campaign to take the Indians' lands. Although it was a great triumph for the Sioux, it was in many ways a hollow victory.

GLOSSARY

Battalion

A group of troops organized to act together.

Bluffs

High, steep banks, cliffs.

Breastwork

A temporary fortification to protect soldiers during battle.

Buckskins

Pants made out of deer skin.

Carcass

The dead body of an animal.

Cavalry

Soldiers mounted on horses.

Centennial

A 100th birthday celebration.

Columns

A long row of soldiers.

Commission

A formal command to act in a certain way or to bring about a certain goal.

Commissioners

Representatives of the government.

Immigrants

Someone who has left his or her home country, in order to settle in another country.

Prospectors

People looking for mineral deposits such as gold or silver.

Recruits

New members of the armed forces.

Regiment

A large military unit made up of a number of battalions.

Reservations

Land set aside for Native Americans by the U.S. government.

Troopers

Cavalrymen, mounted soldiers.

TIMELINE

1868

The Fort Laramie Treaty forbids any white man from setting foot on Paha Sapa—the sacred Black Hills.

1873

Lieutenant Colonel Custer and the Seventh Cavalry come to the northern plains.

1874

Custer leads the Black Hills Expedition where gold is discovered.

1875

The U.S. fails in an attempt to buy the Black Hills from the Indians. The government then orders all hostile Indians to be on the reservation by January 31, 1876, or be considered at war with the United States.

1876

On February 1, the "Indian Problem" is officially handed to the War Department. A three-pronged attack is decided.

On March 17, the first prong of the attack, led by General George Crook, attacks a Sioux and Cheyenne camp on the Powder River.

By spring, Sitting Bull brings together the greatest gathering of Indians ever on the northern plains.

On May 17, the Seventh Cavalry depart from Fort Abraham Lincoln on their summer campaign.

On June 17, at the battle of the Rosebud, General Crook is forced to abandon his end of the campaign.

Custer's last stand takes place on June 25th, and 210 men are killed.

On July 4, the nation celebrates its centennial. News of the battle of the Little Bighorn reaches a shocked nation.

In October, Sioux chiefs finally sign Paha Sapa—the Black Hills—over to the United States government.

FURTHER READING

Ambrose, Stephen E. *Crazy Horse and Custer: The Parallel Lives of Two Warriors*. Landover Hills, Md.: Anchor Books, 1996.

Brininstool, E. A. *Troopers with Custer: Historic Incidents of the Battle of the Little Bighorn*. Mechanicsburg, Pa.: Stackpole Books, 1994.

Donovan, Jim, and Richard S. Wheeler. *Custer and the Little Bighorn: The Man, the Myth, and the Mystery*. Stillwater, Minn.: Voyageur, 2001.

Graham, W. A. *The Story of the Little Bighorn: Custer's Last Fight*. Mechanicsburg, Pa.: Stackpole Books, 1994.

Russell, Jerry L. 1876 *Facts About Custer and the Battle of the Little Bighorn*. New York: Savas, 1999.

Skimin, Robert. *Custer's Luck*. New York: Herodias, 2000.

Sklenar, Larry. *To Hell with Honor: Custer and the Little Bighorn*. Norman: University of Oklahoma Press, 2000.

Utley, Robert. *Cavalier in Buckskin: George Armstrong Custer and the Little Bighorn*. Norman: University of Oklahoma Press, 1991.

INTERNET RESOURCES

George A. Custer

http://www.garryowen.com/

http://www.geocities.com/CollegePark/Classroom/
　　1101/index.html

http://www.georgearmstrongcuster.com/

Sitting Bull

http://www.incwell.com/Biographies/SittingBull.html

http://members.tripod.com/~RFester/lakota.html

http://pages.prodigy.com/custer/sitbul.htm

Crazy Horse

http://www.crazyhorse.org/

http://www.indians.org/welker/crazyhor.htm

http://www.best.com/~maier1/native/memory.htm

Battle of the Little Bighorn

http://www.lbha.org/

http://www.hillsdale.edu/academics/history/Documents/
　　War/America/Indian/1876-BigHorn-Times.htm

http://custerbattle.com

http://www.intuitive.com/sites/cbhma

INDEX

PHOTO CREDITS

2: Little Bighorn Battlefield National Monument/ National Park Service

6: Little Bighorn Battlefield National Monument/ National Park Service

10: West Point Museum Collection/U.S. Military Academy

12-13: North Wind Picture Archives

14: National Archives

18: Denver Public Library

20: Bettmann/Corbis

22: National Archives

25: Reproduced from *A Pictographic History of the Oglala Sioux*, by Amos Bad Heart Bull, text by Helen H. Blish, by permission of the University of Nebraska Press. Plate 130. © 1967 by the University of Nebraska Press. © Renewed 1995 by the University of Nebraska Press

28-29: "Sitting Bull at Little Big Horn," Guy Manning, 40" by 60". Courtesy of El Prado Galleries Inc., Sedona, Arizona.

30: Denver Public Library

35: "Living the Vision," Guy Manning, oil 36" x 72". Courtesy El Prado Galleries, Sedona, Arizona.

36: Hulton/Archive

38: Denver Public Library

40: Little Bighorn Battlefield National Monument/ National Park Service

44-45: Little Bighorn Battlefield National Monument/ National Park Service

46: Reproduced from *A Pictographic History of the Oglala Sioux*, by Amos Bad Heart Bull, text by Helen H. Blish, by permission of the University of Nebraska Press. Plate 146.

49: Little Bighorn Battlefield National Monument/ National Park Service

51: Little Bighorn Battlefield National Monument/ National Park Service

52: Little Bighorn Battlefield National Monument/ National Park Service

53: Little Bighorn Battlefield National Monument/ National Park Service

Cover photos:

(front) Little Bighorn Battlefield National Monument/ National Park Service

(back) West Point Museum Collection/U.S. Military Academy

ABOUT THE AUTHOR

Steve Theunissen is a freelance writer living in Masterton, New Zealand. He is a former personal fitness trainer and has written four books on health and fitness. He is the author of a coming-of-age novel set during the U.S. Civil Rights movement of the early 1960s entitled *Through Angel's Eyes*.